The Navajo Way

The
Postcard
Archive
Series

MUSEUM OF NEW MEXICO PRESS, SANTA FE, NEW MEXICO

A note to the purchaser: The postcards in this book are slightly larger
than standard and require the same postage as first-class mail.

ISBN 0–89013–275-5.

Manufactured in Korea.
10 9 8 7 6 5 4 3 2 1

Design by Deborah Fleig.

Cover: **Navajo riders**. Photo by J.R. Willis. MNM 98187.

Museum of New Mexico Press
P.O. Box 2087
Santa Fe, NM 87504

Preface

Richard Rudisill, Curator of Photographic History, Museum of New Mexico

The Historical Society of New Mexico began collecting pictures soon after its founding in 1859 with catalogue accessions including "Two Photographic views of the Washington Aqueduct" and "An ambrotype of José Calixto Borrego the Mexican dwarf." Although these initial pieces vanished in the disruption of the Civil War, the rebirth of the society in 1880 began steady growth of a collection which was assigned to the Museum of New Mexico in 1977. Since then, overall holdings have reached to half a million items. Subject-matter filing allows researchers to look as much as fourteen decades into New Mexico's past, to view buildings and spaces of Santa Fe or various pueblos, to see past dress styles or work actions, to meet face-to-face the people of earlier days, and to perceive the large and small changes in life otherwise unreachable or forgotten.

Many of these views were made by professionals, upon request or for their own reasons, as entertainment or postcards, for publication or sale. A great number came about simply as personal responses to family events and daily lives that elicted a wish to keep bits of them permanent or to share details with others. A remarkable aspect of the entire collection is that drastic changes in physical circumstances have not been matched by equal shift in the attitudes people hold about why they make pictures or why they enjoy them. Methods of scholarship or social conditions may fluctuate, but most people go on wanting to see how they or their predecessors have appeared and what remains recognizable from a time before. Nostalgia weighs as much as scholarship in such scales of appreciation.

Through its later history, New Mexico stayed current with general photographic practice. By the 1860s and '70s, a few of the studios in the territory were capable of issuing the popular stereoscopic views or producing sunlight enlargements equal with work from "the States." With the advent of the railroad and greater attention from anthropologists, artists, tourists, and traders, the materials and techniques of contemporary eastern work were to be had in Santa Fe or Las Vegas or New Albuquerque, and several major people worked or lived in the region. Ben Wittick, John K. Hillers, Willilam Henry Jackson, and Dana B. Chase were among them.

In the thirty years before World War I, Charles Lummis made hundreds of iron-base blueprints of Indian life, Adam Clark Vroman wrought images in platinum, Aaron Craycraft lugged an 8"x10" view camera into Frijoles Canyon and introduced Dr. Edgar Hewett (archaeologist and founder of the Museum of New Mexico) to the now-famous Tyuonyi Ruins, and Jesse Nusbaum pictured the architecture and rural details of northern New Mexico before recording the new museum's clearing of the Maya site of Quirigua in Guatemala and then going on to carry Pueblo-style structures into the 1915 Panama-California Exposition in San Diego. Then, and later, T. Harmon Parkhurst, H.F. Robinson, and Wesley Bradfield created arrays of negatives reflecting changes in town and Pueblo Indian life. Throughout all that time, amateurs were busy recording whatever the professionals missed to a degree that allows today's Museum of New Mexico Photo Archives to show the richly alive visual heritage of New Mexico.

The
Postcard
Archive
Series

From **The Navajo Way.** © 1995 MUSEUM OF NEW MEXICO PRESS, SANTA FE

Navajo women carding, spinning, and weaving wool
and tending their flock of sheep. MNM 127458.

The Postcard Archive Series

From **The Navajo Way.** © 1995 MUSEUM OF NEW MEXICO PRESS, SANTA FE

Sheepherding, Clyde Peshlakai family.
Photo by Ralph H. Anderson. MNM 130158.

Navajo silversmith Peshlakai Atsidi, also known as "Slim, maker of silver," c. 1885. Photo by Ben Wittick. MNM 16333.

The
Postcard
Archive
Series

Woman and child at the Laguna Pueblo encampment, c. 1935. Photo by T. Harmon Parkhurst. MNM 3240.

The
Postcard
Archive
Series

Merritt Butte, Monument Valley, c. 1935.
Photo by T. Harmon Parkhurst. MNM 71068.

The
Postcard
Archive
Series

From **The Navajo Way.** © 1995 MUSEUM OF NEW MEXICO PRESS, SANTA FE

A young boy meeting a Navajo medicine man,
Alvarado Hotel, Albuquerque. MNM 91481.

The
Postcard
Archive
Series

Trading post. Photo by Betty Woods. MNM 59326.

The
Postcard
Archive
Series

From **The Navajo Way.** © 1995 MUSEUM OF NEW MEXICO PRESS, SANTA FE

Hubbell Trading Post, Ganado, Arizona,
c. 1890. Photo by Ben Wittick. MNM 16480.

PLEASE dont ever
round the car overdog We
have only one that dog take car
of the sheep so if that dog round
do car just stop please the
cotor of dog is yellow and white
when HE Here the car he round
afther so of she do just stop
just chessy it back

Navajo sign put up between Wide Ruins and Chambers. Photo by Sallie Wagner. MNM 3125.

The
Postcard
Archive
Series

From **The Navajo Way.** © 1995 MUSEUM OF NEW MEXICO PRESS, SANTA FE

Navajo women on horseback, 1901.
Photo by Carl N. Werntz. MNM 37595.

From **The Navajo Way.** © 1995 MUSEUM OF NEW MEXICO PRESS, SANTA FE

Sheep watering in a gully, Mormon Valley,
New Mexico, 1936. MNM 5440.

The
Postcard
Archive
Series

From **The Navajo Way.** © 1995 MUSEUM OF NEW MEXICO PRESS, SANTA FE

Navajo women spinning wool, Monument Valley, 1952. Photo by Ralph H. Anderson. MNM 129376.

The
Postcard
Archive
Series

From **The Navajo Way**, © 1995 MUSEUM OF NEW MEXICO PRESS, SANTA FE

Slan-ee-Nez at the camp fire.
Photo by J.R. Willis. MNM 98189.

The
Postcard
Archive
Series

From **The Navajo Way**, © 1995 MUSEUM OF NEW MEXICO PRESS, SANTA FE

Navajo scouts in the Apache campaign of 1886,
c. 1886. Photo by Ben Wittick. MNM 15715.

The
Postcard
Archive
Series

From **The Navajo Way.** © 1995 MUSEUM OF NEW MEXICO PRESS, SANTA FE

Navajo family in a camp, c. 1935.
Photo by T. Harmon Parkhurst. MNM 43137.

The
Postcard
Archive
Series

Sheep grazing near Shiprock, New Mexico. MNM 59022.

The
Postcard
Archive
Series

From **The Navajo Way.** © 1995 MUSEUM OF NEW MEXICO PRESS, SANTA FE

Navajo woman riding a horse, c. 1935.
Photo by T. Harmon Parkhurst. MNM 3207.

Navajo Hogan, c. 1900.
Photo by Wm. H. Simpson. MNM 37675.

The Postcard Archive Series

From **The Navajo Way**, © 1995 MUSEUM OF NEW MEXICO PRESS, SANTA FE

Navajo silversmith. MNM 91455.

The Postcard Archive Series

From **The Navajo Way.** © 1995 MUSEUM OF NEW MEXICO PRESS, SANTA FE

Navajo weaver, c. 1926. MNM 35805.

Navajo women, c. 1935.
Photo by T. Harmon Parkhurst. MNM 3258.

The Postcard Archive Series

From **The Navajo Way**. © 1995 MUSEUM OF NEW MEXICO PRESS, SANTA FE

Navajo women weaving outside of hogan. MNM 44178.

≈

The
Postcard
Archive
Series

≈

From **The Navajo Way.** © 1995 MUSEUM OF NEW MEXICO PRESS, SANTA FE

Navajo jeweler at the Inter-Tribal Indian Ceremonial
in Gallup, New Mexico. Photo by W.T. Mullarky. MNM 27349.

Navajo Woman & baby

Navajo mother and child, c. 1885.
Photo by Ben Wittick. MNM 15711.

The
Postcard
Archive
Series

Shiprock, New Mexico, c. 1935.
Photo by T. Harmon Parkhurst. MNM 22698.

The Postcard Archive Series

From **The Navajo Way.** © 1995 MUSEUM OF NEW MEXICO PRESS, SANTA FE

Navajo riders. Photo by J.R. Willis. MNM 98187.

The
Postcard
Archive
Series

Navajo squaw dance, c. 1935.
Photo by T. Harmon Parkhurst. MNM 3038.

The
Postcard
Archive
Series

From **The Navajo Way.** © 1995 MUSEUM OF NEW MEXICO PRESS, SANTA FE

Navajo bull riding rodeo,
Klagetoh, Arizona, c. 1948. MNM 3134.

The
Postcard
Archive
Series

From **The Navajo Way.** © 1995 MUSEUM OF NEW MEXICO PRESS, SANTA FE

Navajo weaver. Photo by W.T. Mullarky. MNM 91464.